A Completely Unscrupulous Book
Published by Tullulah & Bear
London United Kingdom

2008 by Liesl-Yvette Wilson
All rights reserved

ISBN: 978-0-9559752-5-7

No part of this book may be reproduced, stored in retrieval system, or transmitted by any means, electronic, mechanical, photocopying, recording, or otherwise without written permission.

Fair Horribulous

by

Liesl-Yvette Wilson

For Desperate Antelopes Everywhere

...From All angles and All Heights.

Some like the calm of the Merry-Go-Round.

That is only, of course, because they are bound.

-completely unscrupulous books-
by Liesl-Yvette Wilson

Love Unrequited

A Balloon & A Bear

Around the Corner & on the Left

Evil - or a Plan for World Domination

All Titles are Published by:
Tullulah & Bear Publications uk

www.ingramcontent.com/pod-product-compliance
Lightning Source LLC
Chambersburg PA
CBHW042019150426
43197CB00002B/77